Atwater Kent

An American Story

A. ATWATER KENT
PRESIDENT AND FOUNDER OF THE
ATWATER KENT MFG COMPANY
Philadelphia

Atwater Kent

AN AMERICAN STORY

by NICK LUDINGTON

PALISADES LANDING
PUBLISHING
2016

Printed in the United States of America

First Printing, 2016

ISBN: 978-0-9888986-2-2

Cover & page design: Mary Tiegreen
Cover image: Library of Congress

For Elizabeth Kent Van Alen

KENTS CORNERS CEMETERY
BURIAL PLACE OF ATWATER KENT'S ANCESTORS,
INCLUDING HIS GRANDFATHER, REMEMBER KENT, JR.

THE ANCESTORS

T HE STORY OF ATWATER KENT, LIKE THE STORY OF AMERICA, is westward. It starts on the East Coast, in Vermont where Kent was raised and his forebears are buried in rural Robinson Hill Cemetery, and ends on the West Coast, on a hill in Los Angeles where Kent died in his 32-room Italianate mansion. Projected between is a true-blue American tale of an independent spirit and granite-hard determination creating a great company, important inventions, wealth, art patronage and celebrity. There were bumps along the way. But the lesson is inspiring: Young man! If you work hard, trust your own judgment, take care of your money, and follow your dream without wavering, with a little luck thrown in you can end up with a dozen servants in a Hollywood mansion and movie stars coming for dinner.

Records allow us to begin with 12-year-old Joseph Kent who arrived in Boston aboard the ship "Abigail" in 1634 and went to live with a widowed aunt in Braintree, Massachusetts. Not long after, he moved to Rehobeth, Massachusetts where he, his son Joseph, his grandson John and great grandson Ezekiel passed their lives. These Kents were all law-abiding farmers (none, according to public records, ever went to jail.)

In 1797, Ezekiel's son Remember Kent and others left Rehoboth with their leader, Captain Abdiel Bliss, who fought for three years in the Revolutionary war and took part in the battles at Bunker Hill and Lexington. Joining the westward American adventure, they traveled 200 miles northwest and settled in the newly-organized township of

1

Calais (rhymes with palace), Vermont, a quiet, rural area 10 miles east of Montpelier. Even today the only paved road to Calais is from Montpelier and ends there. Roads leading from Calais elsewhere are stabilized dirt.

When Bliss and Kent arrived, Calais had only a few farms and 175 acres of improved land. The immigration from Massachusetts gave the community new energy and by 1820 the town had 103 houses, nearly 2,000 acres of farmland and 207 students in a population of more than 1,000. Bliss and Remember Kent were prominent in their new community. Bliss served in many township offices and as Calais' representative to the Vermont General Assembly in 1800-1801. Remember Kent, at 23, married Abdiel Bliss' daughter, Rachel. They settled on a farm, one of six cleared for his children by Abdiel Bliss, near a crossroads in Calais later named Kents Corners. Remember also served in town offices and was one of a small group which organized to build the Old West Church. In addition to farming he damned a brook near Kents Corners in 1800 and built a sawmill which was still operating 148 years later. Remember and

KENTS CORNERS TODAY

KENT TAVERN
& HISTORIC MARKER

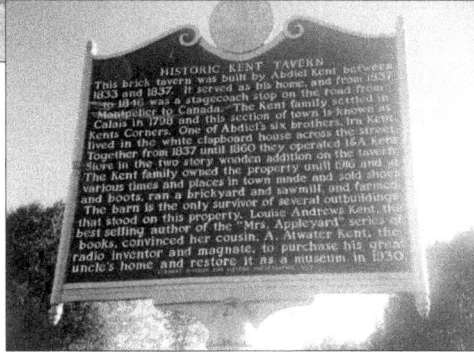

Rachel Bliss Kent had seven children including Abdiel Kent, Ira Kent and Remember Kent, Jr.

Life was simple and close to nature. Wolves were common and the young Kents could hear them howling in the hills nearby. Rachel spun the flax for for the children's socks, shirts and coats. Abdiel Kent told his grandson Dorman that one day his father, Remember, opened the door to look at the weather and in the yard was a large moose. He got his musket, killed the moose with one shot and set the family to skinning the beast, removing the entrails and hanging the meat in the barn. The nine Kents ate moose until April.

Abdiel Kent was the star of the next generation. With his brother Ira, he started and ran an impressive number of business enterprises in and around Kents Corners. At various times Abdiel was a farmer, harness maker, manufacturer of shoes and boots, starch and clapboard, and owner-operator of a general store, tavern, hotel, sawmill and woolen mill. At the same time he served in various town offices and in 1840-41, followed in his grandfather Bliss' footsteps, serving in the Vermont General Assembly.

In 1833, Abdiel built a handsome brick structure at the Kents Corners intersection to serve as a hotel and tavern on the route between Montpelier and Canada. He and brother Ira operated it and an adjoining store until 1860. Ira's descendants ran the store until 1916 when it fell into disuse. In 1930, at the peak of his business success, Atwater Kent bought the property and his son, Atwater Kent, Jr. later contributed funds to help the state of Vermont restore it as a small, country museum. But not many visitors came along the dirt road from Calais to Kents Corners and the museum today is closed and beginning to deteriorate.

Abdiel Kent's energy and entrepreneurial spirit did not appear in his brother, Remember Kent, Jr, who was listed in Calais township records only as a blacksmith and farm laborer. Remember Kent, Jr. married Adelia Tucker in 1833 and the next year Delia, as she was known, gave birth to their eldest son, Prentiss J. Kent. Remember's life, largely unrecorded, did not match his brothers' in accomplishment but after his death, at 82, in 1881 he found a resting place of great peace and beauty. He and Delia are buried with other Kents on Robinson Hill near Kents Corners looking out on a landscape of the Green Mountain State's wooded hills which in fall are painted brilliantly in red, yellow and orange.

The family ambition and drive appeared in Remember Jr.'s son Prentiss. After serving as an apprentice in the home of a Calais merchant named Bancroft, he attended the University of Vermont where he graduated, in 1860, from the University of Vermont Medical School. He quickly signed up as assistant surgeon for the 174th Regiment of New York Volunteers during the civil war. In 1864, Prentiss married Elizabeth Atwater, from a respected family in Burlington, Vermont. After the war he served as doctor in communities in Vermont, Rhode Island and Massachusetts.

ABOVE: THE GRAVES OF REMEMBER AND DELIA KENT

Arthur Atwater Kent

PRENTISS AND ELIZABETH HAD TWO SONS, Osborn and Harry, who died in their first year. On December 3, 1873, Arthur Atwater Kent, their only child who survived past infancy, was born in Smithfield, Rhode Island. Shortly thereafter, the family moved back to Burlington, where Dr. Kent was listed in the 1878 records of the Burlington Medical and Surgical Club as secretary. Elizabeth died in 1896 at 58. Four years later Prentiss, at 66, took a second wife, Clarissa McKnight, known as Clara, of East Montpelier. For some years they lived in Worcester. Prentiss' last years were spent in Montpelier where he and Clara lived in retirement, helped by two of Clara's relatives, until he died in 1919 at 85.

Prentiss and Elizabeth moved around and were often separated. But letters indicate a happy marriage and parents who doted on their only child. In May 1882 Elizabeth wrote from Worcester to Prentiss who was working in Shamrock, R.I.: "I suppose it is unnecessary to say we are lonesome without you … You don't have Libbie to wake you with a kiss, how do you manage?" When Atwater was in his early teens he wrote from summer camp that he attended a dance. "After the first dance was finished I began to feel dazed and knew nothing about where I was and they hustled me off to bed. Old Dr. Bernis came in and said I had an epileptic fit." He said he felt fine the next day. (And never again was there any evidence of epilepsy.) Elizabeth wrote back with obvious concern. "Papa wants to impress strongly on your mind the necessity of avoiding all excitement

EARLIEST KNOWN PHOTOGRAPH
OF ATWATER KENT

and keeping quiet," she wrote. "We have always been careful you know to see that you had plenty of sleep and not too much excitement for one of your nervous temperament." She said Prentiss counseled spending more time in his tent and resting an hour or two each day. "It is important that you take *every precaution* to prevent having any more (unspecified attacks) or it will affect your whole life." This was the beginning of a long tradition of fatherly advice, not always followed.

Arthur Atwater Kent spent his early years in Burlington. In 1881 the Kents moved to Worcester, Massachusetts. Atwater was a restless student. A schoolteacher, Jennie L. Higgins, wrote to Prentiss in 1888 that Atwater "is troubling me somewhat by reading during the time for study also by heedlessness requiring my time and attention." But Atwater showed inventive skill early. As a boy he took apart and re-assembled his mother's sewing machine. In his teens, with the goal of crossing a lake near his home, he built what may have been the first outboard motor, an electric motor driven by a six-cell battery. In 1893 he wrote his mother that he spent all his school vacation hours "down to the shop on electric motors."

FIRST BUSINESS

*I*N 1895 AT AGE 22, Kent entered Worcester Polytechnic Institute in Worcester. He dropped out during the year. Kent was impatient with book learning and laboratories and wanted to concentrate on a business, Kent Electric Mfg. Co., which he founded in 1896 in a one-room plant on Hermon Street in Worcester. Brochures showed that he made sewing machine and other electric motors and electric fans of his own design.

Atwater may have had his father to thank for his extraordinary mechanical imagination. Dr. Prentiss Kent had also been a carpenter and tinkerer. Several pieces of furniture which he made, including a clock with many wooden parts, are still in the family. In a letter to his wife during one separation he talks of using a home-made machine to knit socks and devising a method to make stripes. Apparently worried about doing "women's work" he tells his wife, "Don't say anything to anybody about what is in this letter." In 1902, he wrote his son that he was "tinkering" with a way to run a clock with electricity from a battery. Prentiss worked with Atwater in the Kent Electric Co., perhaps supervising the workmen and doing the bills. After Atwater left Worcester to live in Philadelphia, Prentiss kept up Atwater's workshop. In 1901 a Rhode Island yarn company ordered 2 winding gears and a center shaft. In 1903 Prentiss was producing screws and shafts in Worcester for use in the products Kent was making in Philadelphia.

Kent's small-town origins may have helped his career. The writer Tom

HOME OF PRENTISS AND ELIZABETH KENT
IN BURLINGTON, VERMONT

Wolfe, in an essay on Robert Noyce, the inventor of the semiconductor and founder of Intel, quoted Noyce as saying small-town life, such as his own in Iowa, created inventors. "In a small town you became a technician, a tinker, an engineer, and an inventor, by necessity," Noyce told Wolfe. "In a small town, when something breaks down, you don't wait around for a new part, because it's not coming. You make it yourself."

When Kent's mother died in August 1896 he found out that she had borrowed money on her house to pay for his school fees. Her debts caused a temporary rift between Kent and his father who tried to disclaim the loans saying Elizabeth was unduly influenced by her son. Uncle Henry Atwater, who knew that Kent had not known of the loans, mediated the dispute and that fall, Atwater re-entered WPI. His uncle Edgar Atwater wrote him from Burlington in September to congratulate him. "We were all pleased that you had complied with your mother's wishes and resumed your studies. "She cannot now share your joys and sorrows," Uncle Edgar wrote. "But I firmly believe she is still your guardian angel, watching your every act... You can never know her inward thoughts and feelings, the impassioned love and affection for her boy ... but I believe you have started on the right path."

Atwater Kent told family members later in life that he loved his mother and had trouble getting along with his father. But the only known serious problem between them was the rift after Elizabeth's death which was patched up within months. Their correspondence was always correct and often friendly right up to Prentiss' death. It showed no rancor but contrasting personality types: Prentiss careful and conservative, Atwater venturesome.

Probably for his mother's sake, Kent tried again for part of a school year in 1896-1897, studying math and science, particularly electricity as he continued his electrical business. But he dropped out for good in 1897.

The grave marker of Prentiss and Elizabeth Kent in Burlington, Vermont

The parting between Kent and Worcester Tech was amicable. Kent served on the board of the college from 1926 to 1931. And WPI later named its electrical engineering laboratory building after Kent, who left the school a six-figure gift in his will. When the laboratories were dedicated to Kent in 1981 the school noted in the program: "When he left WPI, he could have continued on as a special student if he were willing to devote more time to his studies and less time tinkering with his experiments. That unappetizing proposition, combined with his even-then growing business interests, made his choice simple."

The WPI yearbook of 1899, the first class Kent would have graduated with, also reported that Kent neglected book learning for business. "Mr. Kent, of the Kent Electric Co., sojourned with us for the space of one term, during which time he held the purse of the class (treasurer)," the yearbook wrote. "Either the duties and cares of this office were too burdensome, or his outside electrical work too engrossing, for he failed to appear at recitations after the mid-year exams. More confident than ever in his ability to bluff, he entered the class of 1900 in the following year (1896) and, of course, his relations with us became more or less indirect. His bluffs worked well for a time (as would be expected in a class of bluffers), but they didn't 'score points' on the exams, and now Arthur devoted most of his time to the affairs of his company. A good natured fellow with a pleasant smile, he may be seen at his best Sunday evenings at Piedmont Church receiving the offering and (he fondly imagines) the admiration of the young ladies."

LADIES MAN

T HIS PERIOD, STARTING IN 1899, provides a first look at Kent as romantic, a trait he carried to his death. Kent was a man who loved dances, the best place to meet girls in that restricted era. He met many.

In 1899, Kent got a letter from Worcester while on a sales trip to New York in which "Anna" told him "I miss you very much indeed. I miss your quick step, your cheery voice and your dear face from the bottom of my heart ... Goodnight my darling."

At the same time he was seeing and corresponding with a girl from Beverly, Mass. with connections in Worcester named Mary Hoxie Ryder. He gave her a gold heart marked "MHR" to hang on her wrist. " She made "My Dear Arthur" a box of fudge. They may even have had an unofficial engagement as Kent's Cousin Edith Atwater wrote him on Jan. 14, 1900 sending love to "the young lady to whom you are engaged."

Nellie Mae Bryant and "Gertrude" of Lebanon, N.H. made fudge for him too. Mary Richard invited him for a weekend of horseback riding in Connecticut. A young woman named Ella Carr wrote him to thank him for photos reminding her of a *pleasant* summer."

A proper young woman in Boston, Marie Paul, sent him an engraved invitation to a dance given by her family and in a letter, answering his request for a photo, requested his photo "as soon as possible." He also sent a photo to Miss Florence Taylor, a Boston girl attending The Misses Ely's School in New York City. "It is very good indeed of you and a very fine picture," she wrote. She told Kent, who was going to a sporting event without her, "Don't forget me and don't take any other girl."

There were letters from other girlfriends: Muriel and Stella, Worcester girls, Lilian Rogers, a girl he met in Brooklyn on a sales trip, Margaret Smith in Boston, Florence Louise Fuller of Woodstock, Vt., Helen Manning at Smith College in Northampton, and in particular Betty Macomber, an intelligent, well-read, whist-playing cooking teacher, actress and golfing enthusiast in Newton Centre, Mass. Betty Macomber was clearly one of Kent's important girl friends.

THE YOUNG INVENTOR, C. 1896

Kent Electric Manufacturing Co.

HE LETTERHEAD OF THE KENT ELECTRIC MANUFACTURING Co. announced that the firm made "Alternating Current Fans, Alternating Sewing Machine Motors, The Celebrated Drum Armature, Battery Motors, Dynomos (sic), Water Motors." It boasted, "We Make a Speciality of Light Power and Build Special Motors." At some point in 1899 Kent devised the "Amperia" a game which used a battery and small electric motor to spin color wheels. He attempted to sell the toy on trips around New England and even to New York but the product flopped. However, that year Kent was doing well enough in business to take a three-week vacation at the Cliff Hotel in North Scituate Beach, Mass. He lived in a boarding house on Main Street in Worcester, with a roommate, Herbert Hirschberg, a shoe store owner. Kent was a member of the Worcester Boat Club, rowed in shells and canoes on the lake and raced in sailboats when he got the chance, a start in a pastime which he would later indulge in extravagantly.

A Kent Electric Mfg. Co. brochure of 1899 showed that Kent had turned his attention to the most difficult problem facing the gasoline engine, which had started to replace steam engines, igniting the fuel-air mixture in the engine cylinder so the engine would run smoothly. He devised the "Kent Gas Engine Igniter" for stationary engines.

The Electrical World and Engineer magazine reported in early 1900 that Kent sold his business to Kendrick and Davis in Lebanon, New Hampshire and went to work for the firm which made toys and electrical equipment. Kent also provided his designs including the gas engine igniter which, after one modification, Kendrick and Davis called "the greatest igniter on earth." He also sold Kendrick and Davis a half interest in an electric top, an improvement on the "Amperia," toy which he patented in March 1901. He lived in Lebanon and began traveling to sell electrical equipment. In 1900 Kent wrote, and Kendrick and Davis published, a small, 32-page pamphlet, "Electrical Units for Boys" which explained in clear and simple terms amperes, ohms, volts and watts and described the workings of electrical motors. In the preface Kent wrote, "I have been asked so many times, 'What is a volt?' and 'What is an ampere?' that I feel quite sure that this little work will find a place among those who wish to

KENT'S PAMPHLET, PUBLISHED IN 1900 BY KENDRICK AND DAVIS

know something about electricity and are not advanced far enough in mathematics to study a more technical work, or are too busy to read a more lengthy work on the subject." The clear style and organization of the pamphlet give an idea of Kent's orderly mind and clarity of thought which, allied with self-discipline, energy and single-minded purpose, propelled him, in the Horatio Alger tradition, to business success.

In early 1901 Kent joined the Holtzer-Cabot Electric Co. in Boston who sent him to be their sales representative in Philadelphia for the company's electric motors and dynamos. After trying several boarding houses, Kent, in November 1901 settled in a room at the corner of Broad and Spruce "one of the best locations in the city," he wrote his father. Room and board cost $8.50 a week. He decided Philadelphia was an ideal place to start a new business. "I found I did not like working for other people," he wrote in a 1938 memo to his son Atwater about his early business years. "I wanted to be my own boss and receive the full benefits of my own work." The 1938 memo, (referred to thus in later pages) was found among Atwater, Jr.'s papers after he died in 1988. It was only a few pages long, but valuable as virtually the only source of information from Kent himself on important aspects of his business career.

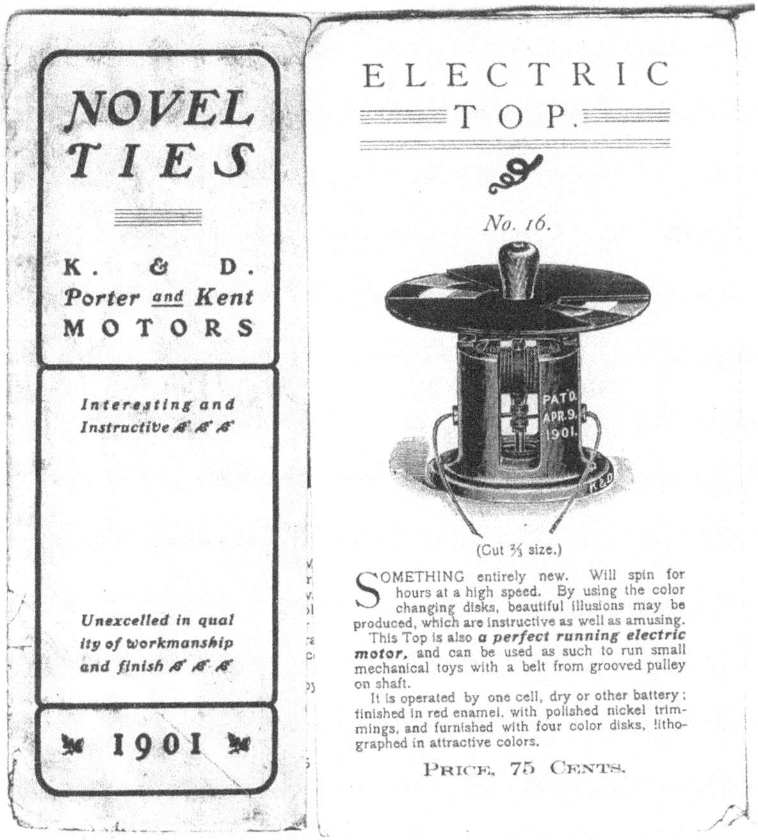

NOVEL TIES

K . & D .
Porter and *Kent*
M O T O R S

Interesting and
Instructive

Unexcelled in qual
ity of workmanship
and finish

❧ 1 9 0 1 ❧

ELECTRIC
TOP.

No. 16.

(Cut ⅔ size.)

SOMETHING entirely new. Will spin for hours at a high speed. By using the color changing disks, beautiful illusions may be produced, which are instructive as well as amusing.
This Top is also *a perfect running electric motor,* and can be used as such to run small mechanical toys with a belt from grooved pulley on shaft.
It is operated by one cell, dry or other battery; finished in red enamel, with polished nickel trimmings, and furnished with four color disks, lithographed in attractive colors.

PRICE, 75 CENTS.

AN AD FOR KENT'S ELECTRIC TOY TOP

ATWATER KENT MANUFACTURING CO.

*H*is top had been selling well. In early 1902 he received a royalty check for $50. and, according to a letter from F. Kendrick, Kendrick and Davis was "making preparations for a big run on the top next year." Using the top royalties and about $250 from savings, he founded the Atwater Kent Mfg. Works in 1902 to assemble intercom telephones from parts ordered from others. "It will either make or break me," he wrote his father in April 1902, saying he planned to burn his bridges and quit his salaried position with Holtzer-Cabot's Philadelphia agent, Novelty Electric Co. Prentiss replied with characteristic worry about the move. He said he did not want to discourage Atwater, "but you know you and I do things a little differently. I like to keep myself firmly on my feet while you would work more on anticipation." Prentiss said he did not want Atwater "to get in debt as you were here" (in Worcester).

Prentiss' paternal interference was constant. As Atwater geared up for his new venture, his father chided him for going back to smoking cigarettes. "It is a perfectly well established pathological fact that no tobacco user is so good a man in any position as he would be without it," Prentiss wrote. He urged his 30-year-old son to "take a little of the time you spend on society" and study the matter. Even much later in 1915, when Kent was rich and well established in Philadelphia, his father wrote, "You have a perfect right to be proud, and I am, but don't let it puff you up too much for we hear about it bursting people sometimes."

Kent later expressed pride in never having had to borrow for his ventures. But he wrote his father in April that getting through the first six months "will be a tight squeeze." F. Kendrick of Kendrick and Davis turned down a request from Kent for a loan of $200 to help him get started. He appealed to his father for $300 in May saying the stores were enthusiastic about the phones but that he needed money to buy enough parts. "I hate very much to ask you to loan me any money as you have always been so adverse to lending me any but I have got to do it or give up the fine business that I have started … it means so much to me." Prentiss sent $100 and said, "I hope it will help you out. I want to see you succeed." Atwater later wrote him that the check was a "godsend" without which he would have certainly failed. He paid it back in 1904 with interest.

THE MONOPLEX PHONE

KENT GAVE UP MOST SOCIAL EVENTS ("It's a hard time of year to shut myself away from my friends but I am willing to gain my ends," he wrote Prentiss) and set up business in two small rented rooms at 116 North 7th Street. The telephone venture was based on Kent's belief that he could put together a decent, practical product more efficiently and cheaply than others. He wrote his father that he could "compete with the world. I am second to nobody!" He hired two workmen, printed business stationary with a large "AK" in a circle as a logo, and marketed the "Monoplex Telephone" in a light blue brochure as "A first class moderate priced telephone" costing $5 a pair. He sold 200 phones in the first two weeks, 50 of them to the huge John Wanamaker department store. Business slowed down in the summer and Kent had

Monoplex Telephones

Price, $2.50 Each

Manufactured by
ATWATER KENT
MANUFACTURING WORKS
112 NORTH SIXTH STREET,
PHILADELPHIA

to move his plant to a loft at 112 North 6th St. which, according to one account, had cracks so large between the floorboards, Kent did not need a dustpan when he swept. He later was quoted as telling a friend: "I started at one end of my space and swept to the other. But by the time I had reached the other end, there was no dust left to pick up. It had all gone through the cracks in the floor. That's why I always wanted to be on top – so nobody can sweep any dirt on my head."

Kent turned down an investor who wanted to

7TH AVENUE CREW. MONOPLEX AND POCKET METER
MANUFACTURERS. ATWATER KENT, FAR RIGHT

put $5,000 in the business because he wanted to keep full control even though he was short of capital. In the fall sales picked up and in January 1903 Atwater wrote his father that he had sold 1,000 phones since October and that none had been returned. He introduced new models of six-station and ten-station intercoms for factories or offices at $4 per phone. And he bought a Smith Premier typewriter on installments and a second-hand desk for $3.

Because of competition, the phone business was "discouraging but not entirely a failure," Kent said in the 1938 memo to his son, Atwater, Jr. Kent kept a penciled record of his first-year results. He reported net earnings of $3,000 of which he paid $1,500 to himself as salary and set aside $1,500 to promote future sales.

THE KENT POCKET METER

NOT SATISFIED WITH THE TELEPHONE PROSPECTS, Kent invented a battery tester, the Kent Pocket Meter, for use mainly on automobiles whose sales had started to grow rapidly. A marketing circular boasted "This is without doubt the most convenient and complete battery tester on the market." It was not an invention but a patentable improvement because it was portable and easy to use. Kent found profitable sales immediately. Prentiss wrote his son in October 1903, "Glad of the success of the meter. Hope you make it a real prosperity but am very sorry to have the telephone fall back." But when Kent wrote in 1904 with new hopeful estimates Prentiss replied, "experience has shown that you are apt to be too optimistic." He urged his son to save for a rainy day and not invest too much in the business. Prentiss, as usual, was too pessimistic.

"KENT POCKET METERS"
are standard and most reliable
Volt Ammeters
0-6 V.,0.30 A.
Price,$6.00
0-5 V., 20 A.
Price $6.00
Atwater Kent Mfg. Wks.
"Dead Beat" Accuracy Guaranteed
Volt Meters
0-6 V. Price $4.00
Am. Meters
0-20 A. Pr. $4.00
0-30 A. Pr. $4.00
106 N. 6th St.
Philadelphia.

Kent said in the 1938 memo to his son, "I had enough business experience to realize that a good thing never lasts very long, so I worked hard to make as much money out of these meters as I could before the inevitable competition came in." The meter business provided him with healthy profits for about four years and these profits allowed him to invent and develop an ignition system for automobiles which, he said, "was really my great success in life."

22

THE UNISPARKER

*I*N 1903 KENT HAD BOUGHT HIS FIRST AUTOMOBILE, a one-cylinder Jeffrey Rambler, taking it in trade for a number of his battery testers. (Prentiss, in his gloomy way, told Atwater he thought the car dealer got the best of the deal.) Kent was dissatisfied with the ignition system, according to an interview in 1928 with the Dayton, Ohio Journal, and this frustration drove him to improve it. "It was bad enough when it didn't miss," Kent said in the interview, "hammering everyone in the back with every explosion of the engine, but when the vibrator (most cars then used a vibrator spark coil) stuck it was awful – especially going up hill." Kent had turned his inventive mind to ignition systems earlier with the "gas engine igniter" he designed for Kendrick and Davis. And a November 1901 letter to Kent from Edmund Cellison, chief engineer at the Union Motor Truck Co. in Philadelphia, thanks Kent "for your interest taken in my experiment with the jump spark ignition in connection with the Holtzer-Cabot magneto ... In case you have any ignition apparatus you wish to try on gasoline engines privately, you can call on me any time."

It is not known what role Cellison's experiments played in Kent's invention. But Kent moved into a larger area on Arch Street and, in 1905, introduced the revolutionary "Unisparker," an automobile ignition system, superior to anything on the market at the time, which integrated the series of weak sparks in existing systems into a single, hot spark. The Kent Unisparker combined contact points, condenser, centifrugal

ADVERTISEMENT, C. 1912

advance mechanism and distributor into a compact unit. Kent took out a number of patents which protected the ignition system until 1924.

Kent's son Atwater, Jr. said his father had told him that after the Unisparker was announced, a man came to the door of Kent's factory loft and found Kent holding a broom. "Would you take me to Mr. Kent," the man asked and was surprised when the young sweeper said "I am Mr. Kent." The visitor was a buyer from the Ford Motor Co. who placed a substantial order for the Unisparker, launching the invention. The Unisparker design was used in most autos until the adoption of electronic ignition. For the invention, Kent was given the John Scott Legacy Medal and Premium by the Franklin Institute of Philadelphia in 1914.

The year after introducing the Unisparker, Kent estimated in a letter to his father that in a year he would sell 800 of them at $60 each, with a profit to him of $10 each. He said "They" (presumably an auto company or companies) were thinking taking about 500 larger models of the invention for larger cars on which Kent would profit $20 each. The Unisparker became original equipment on many makes including Peerless, Maxwell, Franklin and Hupmobile. It was also sold to be retrofitted on Fords and Packards. He moved into a larger factory space at 42-46 North 6th St.

Installing the

ATWATER KENT

Ignition System Type "H"

ON THE

Ford

Type H Unisparker Mounted on Ford Motor

NOTE: The Atwater Kent System is made in two forms—Type "K-2" with Automatic Spark Advance — Type "H" without the Automatic Advance Feature.

ATWATER KENT MFG. WORKS
4937 Stenton Ave., Philadelphia, Pa.

SOCIAL STATUS

*P*HYSICALLY, KENT DID NOT ATTRACT ATTENTION. Of medium height and average physique, he was pleasant looking rather than handsome. He did not rely on his looks to get ahead but was aware of the importance of making a good impression. He always dressed and groomed himself carefully, brushing his thin hair straight back from his forehead. He was not a great wit or commanding conversationalist. But he clearly understood that a good listener can be just as popular as the exhibitionist "life of the party." Kent was impeccably polite and conveyed genuine interest in what others were saying. He absorbed what he needed for business or social progress and let the rest filter through. Kent was looking for useful information or connections, not advice. He made up his own mind. His one impressive physical feature was his glance. Kent's eyes were the eyes of a falcon or a great athlete, focused intensely on the task at hand, in his case not a plump songbird or a six-foot putt for millions of dollars, but how to create and sell a product. The decisive eyes reflected his self-confidence. He made rapid decisions and followed through without paying attention to doubters like his father. Kent's business success in Philadelphia was matched by a rise in his social fortunes. In 1901 Kent's father, worried about how his son was acclimating in a big city, wrote from Vermont, "Am wondering how you are getting on in society. I think of it a good deal." In another letter, Prentiss wrote that he could not sleep because of worry about his son's ambitious new life and predicted darkly that Atwater might get ahead of himself and into money trouble. "Arthur, I am so anxious for you, to have you succeed, have you get up in the world in a true and worthy sense," he wrote. He warned against the "froth and frivolities of society," and said "A wish to mingle in the 'best' i.e. wealthy society is very laudable but much too expensive to be indulged in by persons of ordinary means. Better wait until the means are greater ... why do you allow yourself to be so dependent upon that kind of society for happiness? I wish you might free yourself from it and be a slave no longer." And Kent himself told his son, Atwater, Jr., in the 1938 memo, that when he came to Philadelphia, "I was undoubtedly green and knew nobody and had to make my own way socially."

Prentiss need not have worried. Kent's business advances supported his social life and there is no indication of overspending. Whatever handicap Kent's rural Vermont upbringing might have been to mingling in polite society, he surmounted it easily. He had the natural ability to make friends and get along with people, and he worked at it. Invitations and flirtatious notes testify to Kent's busy social life in Philadelphia starting in 1901. A letter to his father gave his social schedule for two weeks before Christmas that year and he had at least one event every day, sometimes two or more including parties, dances, calls on ladies, football games lunches and dinners.

HIS ONE IMPRESSIVE PHYSICAL FEATURE WAS HIS GLANCE. KENT'S EYES WERE THE EYES OF A FALCON OR A GREAT ATHLETE, FOCUSED INTENSELY ON THE TASK AT HAND, IN HIS CASE NOT A PLUMP SONGBIRD OR A SIX-FOOT PUTT FOR MILLIONS OF DOLLARS, BUT HOW TO CREATE AND SELL A PRODUCT. THE DECISIVE EYES REFLECTED HIS SELF-CONFIDENCE.

Kent wrote Prentiss in 1902 "People say they never saw anybody become acquainted as rapidly as I do ... Sometimes I think I am reaching a limit for a practical acquaintanceship for I can hardly do justice to those that I do know. However I always make it a point to give the greatest attention and all of the time that I can. On the other hand, sometimes I think that I want to keep on increasing my acquaintance for I find no harm in it and Phila (delphia) apparently offers an inexhaustible supply of nice people." He said his father would forgive his conceit if he followed his son for a week and heard remarks made to him about his popularity. Kent said sometimes these compliments were boring because he had to be ready with "some humble remark." Kent also told his father that he was working to improve his diction by reading aloud 15 minutes each evening "enunciating very distinctly and with as firm a voice as I can muster up." He said it helped him greatly in conversation, not only socially, but in business where he was better able to make another person pay attention to him while "still giving him the impression that I am following him."

Betty Macomber, the lively girlfriend who pined for Kent from Newton Centre, Massachusetts, saw him slipping away in the big city. "Isn't it just the kind of life you like, meeting a lot of people and having a lot going on?" she wrote in October, 1901. And in March, 1902: "Have you gotten to the silk hat stage on Sundays since you have been in Philadelphia? You are the greatest one for keeping up with the latest wrinkle."

Notes to Kent during the early Philadelphia period survive from a dozen young women. He escorted dates to musical concerts and dances including the "Clover Ball." A male friend, Ralph White, who had left town on a vacation, wrote to Kent, "You must have your hands full with so many girls." Kent said that he learned to play Whist, a card game similar to Bridge. "I played a pretty fair game and would often win a prize in a Whist club to which I belonged," he told Atwater in the 1938 memo. He also took up ping-pong which was popular among young people. In March 1904 he joined the posh Merion Cricket Club in Haverford paying dues of $30 per year.

The most serious romance during 1903 and 1904 was with Theodoro Sharp, a dark-haired 20-year-old from a wealthy family. Kent told his father in March 1904 that Theo was "more adapted for me than any girl I ever saw." But in May he seemed to sense that the relationship would fail. He wrote his father that he liked her "immensely" but that she blew hot and cold and he predicted that "it will all blow over." There were hints that her family may not have approved of the young businessman. In July Theo wrote Atwater that the romance should end. She said she realized that he "didn't care in the way I thought you did. I only hope you will forget me entirely." And two weeks later: "As I said before we should let the whole matter drop. I know we could never get along together."

ATWATER KENT AND MABEL LUCAS
IN ATLANTIC CITY BEFORE THEIR MARRIAGE
IN 1906

MARRIAGE

*I*N 1906 HE CAPPED HIS SOCIAL SUCCESS by marrying Mabel Lucas, from a family whose bank accounts had dwindled but who maintained a respected place in Philadelphia society. He met Mabel, who lived with her widowed mother and three younger siblings in a small house in the fashionable suburb of Bryn Mawr, about the time he broke up with Theo Sharp in 1904. In early November he sent her violets and she said she "never in all my life appreciated anything so much." Next month he called and also sent tickets for a light opera. ("Really in all my life I never heard of such thoughtfulness.") In 1905 they spent time together in the summer in Maine. She thanked him in a February 1906 letter for taking the time to pick out a Valentine "when you are so busy. I never heard of such a man!" She also thanked him in another letter for giving her mother a subscription to the magazine "Town Topics." "What a lot of pleasure you give to this family," she wrote.

Knowing his father could not send a lavish wedding present, Kent sent Prentiss a check for $100 and asked Prentiss to make out his own check for $100 and send it to Mabel as a wedding gift. Prentiss slyly exhibited his pride by also sending Atwater a separate check from his own funds. The amount is unknown but Atwater wrote his father that he was as pleased with his check as Mabel was with hers. He was also pleased with a $1,000 check from Mabel's grandmother and 97 gifts from Lucas family and friends.

The Lucas family seemed delighted with Mabel's catch. Mabel's grandmother, in addition to her $1,000 check, sent Kent a letter three weeks before the marriage saying, "You have seemed for a long time my very own grandson and I could not love you more if this relationship had always existed." Mabel's sister Natalie also sent Kent friendly letters addressing him as "Dear Brother."

They were married May 29, 1906 and took a week's honeymoon to Niagara Falls and then toured auto factories in New England in Kent's new Packard to sell the Unisparker. Their first summer of married life was spent with Mabel in a rented house at Cape May on the New Jersey shore with Kent commuting back and forth to Philadelphia five times a week. Their first home was a comfortable two-story Victorian-style house at 500 41st St. at Baltimore Ave. in West Philadelphia. In 1907 they moved to a remodeled house at 2048 Pine Street, nearer the factory in center city and a year later to 2227 Spruce St. Starting in 1908 with Atwater, Jr. they produced three children. Elizabeth was born in 1911 and Virginia in 1915. They adopted an infant, Prentiss, in 1923.

When she and Kent were married, Mabel was a popular young woman with a wide circle of good friends in Philadelphia society. She was as tall as Kent with appealing, dark looks and a tiny waist. After her children were born she grew into a more matronly figure. Her face and demeanor invited trust and confidences. Mabel may have failed in attracting from her husband the generous, unqualified, open love she gave him. But she became a magnetic center of her family, a mother-confessor, to whom children and grandchildren could talk openly, sharing their problems without fear of criticism.

Some stuffy members of Philadelphia society accused Kent of being a social climber. Kent himself was open and realistic about his social ambitions. In a May 1904 letter to his father, he said he thought that by virtue of being able to buy an automobile and being "extremely patient" he was "being thrown in with a certain class of people. I am working myself into the 400 of Philadelphia." Kent said, "I was not killing myself to do it, but just at present a good wave has come and is carrying me along

in good shape." He mentioned being asked along on a party given on a 120-foor yacht by a member of the Wetherill family, "one of the leaders of Philadelphia society. "They give a great many parties of this kind and I am told that I am going to be invited again. I hope so."

Years later at a dinner party, Cassandra Ludington, one of Kent's granddaughters sat next to a man who, not aware of his dinner partner's connection, spoke of Kent as a low-born arriviste who had bought his way into polite society. "But," the man continued. "I understand he had two lovely daughters." The granddaughter stunned him redfaced by replying, "Yes, one of them is my mother, sitting over there."

Kent could be touchy about his upbringing. He chided his father in 1907 for writing to Mabel with details of his simple early life. "Don't you know that I said that Mabel could not understand our way of living and she would call it absolute poverty. Your letter made her very blue as she felt that I was almost a beggar before I came to Philadelphia."

Though the marriage broke up 30 years later, it started as a love match between a warm-hearted socialite and a driven young entrepreneur glowing with his first successes. "Dearest Old Snooks," she addressed him in a love letter a few months before they married.

Kent traveled frequently in their early married years, selling the Unisparker, and Mabel recognized his workaholic nature. Included with a letter just before their marriage was a cartoon she had drawn showing, in the first box, "the world's greatest inventor" busy at his factory personally selling his auto products. The second box has him rushing home asking, "am I in time for the ceremony?" And in the third box they are kneeling in front of the minister.

There are gentle hints at jealousy. In 1913 she wrote, "Do you get lonely dearie? No you don't for as you say the ladies and you get very chummy. Now don't get too "Western" out there." In another letter she told him to stay away from the "pier ladies." She constantly pestered him to know what he was doing in the evenings of his business trips. "Do try and be good for your little wife," she wrote. Her fears surfaced in a "nightmare" she wrote about in 1914. "I dreamed at the Fitler dance that you wouldn't dance with me and went off with some girl and were making love to her at a terrific rate."

His letters to her have disappeared. But Kent expressed delight with his marriage. He wrote his father in August 1906 that married life was great. "Mabel and I are just as happy as can be. She truly is a congenial girl. Everybody likes her." Mabel knew most of the "nicest people of Philadelphia," Kent said. "I feel very fond of her. We are together all of the time and seldom have any trouble. Once I stayed out overnight on a boat on business about the 'generator' (the Unisparker) and she did not like that and what differences we have are usually of that kind." After two pages about his marriage, Kent got back to business with five more pages about the Unisparker.

FIRST FORTUNE

ENT'S ENTHUSIASM WAS WELL GROUNDED. Business was going well. In February of 1907 he had 42 workers. They were paid about $12 a week or $600 a year, allowing for handsome profits. On Dec 31, 1908, Kent sent his father a letter reporting on that year's results. Gross income was $104,800 "which is double what I did last year." Expenses, including capital improvements in machinery and plant, were about $80,000. The profit, therefore, was $24,000. Kent said he took a salary of $10,000 and put the rest back into the business. Kent could not resist a dig at his father's constant, conservative carping about saving. "You have always talked to me about laying money aside in the bank. But could you ask for any better results from an investment of my yearly earnings than putting them in a business that brings me such handsome profits as these?" In June 1910 Kent wrote his father that he was shipping Unisparkers at a rate of $30,000 a month and employed 100 workers. For the first time, the letter was typed by a secretary.

He moved his production facility in 1912 to yet larger quarters on Stenton Avenue and added an electric horn he had patented in 1911 and automobile lighting systems to his line of products. A 1912 brochure advertised that the Unisparker, "A Scientific Ignition System for Automobiles, Motor Boats, Stationary Engines and Aeroplanes," was in use as regular equipment by 20 manufacturers of cars and motors.

By 1912, his success with the Unisparker allowed the Kents to move from Philadelphia to the suburban Main Line where they rented a house in Wynnewood for $150 a month. The next year, the house burned down and they looked for another. Mabel wrote Kent in 1913 that she hoped that at his club he "would meet some nice (euphemism for socially connected) men that could help us climb that fool Main Line ladder!" In 1914 they were renting a house in Rosemont. The next year they finished the climb. Kent bought a seven-acre property in Ardmore. They began renting a summer house in Kennebunkport, Maine where the Lucas family had summered for years. They became a two-car family with a Chalmers and a Buick. "It is wonderful to think of you making so much that we can have so many luxuries," Mabel wrote to Kent in 1914.

In May, 1919, Kent's father died in Montpelier of complications from liver cancer and the cautious fatherly advice stopped. Kent traveled to Vermont for the funeral and accompanied his father's body from Montpelier to Burlington where he was buried with his first wife, Elizabeth, and their two infants. All the family, except Atwater, rest in a now-shabby neighborhood of Burlington. They lie beneath a modest marble obelisk in the Elmwood Avenue Cemetery which reads, "Prentiss J. Kent, 1834-1919, His Wife Elizabeth M. Kent, 1838-1896, Children Osborn, Harry." Tiny blocks of granite with their initials mark the graves of the infant boys. Locks of hair from Osborn and Harry were found in papers passed down in the family.

As the United States entered World War One, the Army Ordinance Department chose the Atwater Kent Mfg. Co. to design and manufacture panoramic gunsights for the new Browning machine guns allowing the weapons to lay down a controlled barrage against a fixed area. The army also chose Kent to make fuse setters, to time the explosion of artillery shells, and other sophisticated fire control instruments called clinometers and theodolites. After the war, the army attested that Kent had produced devices with design features superior to the specifications given the company.

In the postwar period, along with other businessmen, Kent faced a national economic slump. He had 125 workers but business was slow.

STENTON AVENUE FACTORY WHERE PARTS FOR
KENT'S UNISPARKER WERE PRODUCED

More and more autos were being sold with the ignition system built in, diminishing the need for his products. Kent was helped by his 25 patents (a number which eventually grew to 93), and he was earning royalties on many of them.

Kent said in the 1938 memo to his son that the Unisparker allowed him to build a fortune of three million dollars by 1919, before he switched to radio manufacturing. He said that his profit margin on the Unisparkers and other products was about 35%, high for manufacturing and that he achieved this margin by working hard himself, hiring few administrators and running a no-frills operation. "At that time I was considered by business men quite an unusual person as I had never borrowed a dollar from the banks and I had built my business up entirely from my own earnings and I always paid my bills as soon as they were presented," Kent wrote. In 1920, having accumulated a fortune, he went abroad for the first time and considered retiring. But in 1922, seeing a new field of great opportunity, Kent turned to radio.

THE YOUNG MARRIEDS,
WITH ELIZABETH AND ATWATER, JR., C. 1918

THE RADIO BOOM

*A*YEAR OR SO AFTER THE WAR Kent had received an order for 10,000 headphones for use with the new craze, wireless radio. Marine and military wireless technology for point-to-point communication was first adapted for amateur ham radio operators, then for a general use, entertaining and informing the general public. The first radio station, KDKA, was put into operation by Westinghouse in Pittsburgh on November 2 1920, broadcasting the Harding-Cox presidential election returns. Kent alertly saw the potential of manufacturing radio sets, and was unfazed by monopolizing attempts of the giant "radio group" led by the Radio Corporation of America (RCA) and including Westinghouse, General Electric and AT&T.

Earnings from the Unisparker allowed him to get started. He first started building radio components, including transformers, viometers, switches, tube sockets and sealed amplifier units. He built his first complete radio set himself, by hand in his attic, and started assembling complete sets in late 1922. The Atwater Kent Mfg. Co. was ready, in spring, 1923, with two models (Model 5 and Model 10) of "open sets" or breadboards, a varnished board with the tubes and tuning apparatus fixed on top.

The Atwater Kent

UNISPARKER

A Scientific Ignition System
for
Automobiles, Motor Boats,
Stationary Engines and Aeroplanes

ATWATER KENT MFG WORKS
42-50 NORTH SIXTH STREET
PHILADELPHIA

Kent believed that getting into radio without any technical experience in the field was difficult and that good technical men were hard to find because of competition. And he realized that the big profits would be made in the early years, before competition became intense. "I buckled down to hard work, giving up my vacations in the winter and taking them only every other week in the summer," he said in the 1938 memo. "Business went forward by leaps and bounds."

Kent sold 6,628, five-tube Model 10 sets the first year. His timing was perfect; he had entered radio just as it was beginning its golden age. Newspapers, which today carry entire sections on television stars and programming, began publishing special pages on radio broadcast stars, programs and manufactured products. The number of radio sets manufactured in the United States grew 1,000 % between 1923 and 1925. By 1927 there were 7 million sets in homes in the United States and 700 radio stations had been licensed.

According to Ralph Williams, a historian of the radio industry, "Kent brought the best minds of his time into his organization to do radio design, factory operation, marketing and product advertising." Williams said he was careful of his company's reputation, making radios of high quality and reliability and aiming sales at the middle class.

Kent first expanded his operation into adjacent buildings on Stenton Avenue but by 1924 he had run out of space. He continued to make auto ignition systems on Stenton Avenue but bought a 20-acre tract on Wissahicken Avenue and, for $2 million, built 11 acres of plant space. He later bought more adjacent land and, by 1929, had expanded plant space to 32 acres. To walk around the plant building was a trip of 1.5 miles. Williams wrote that "Kent wanted a factory that not only built his radios but also enhanced his image as a major entrepreneur in the American business scene." The plant, highly advanced for its time, combined engineering laboratories, commercial offices, and headquarters staff offices with the manufacturing space. At 1929 dedication ceremonies, Kent spoke, revealing his continuing zest for progress. He said, "the

ABOVE: THE IMPRESSIVE ATWATER KENT
FACTORY ON WISSAHICKEN AVENUE;
LEFT: AD, SEPTEMBER 1929

radio business is something which is constantly changing and constantly moving forward. To me this is very inspiring and stimulating. I could not be happy doing the same thing every day in the same way, cut and dried to order. I like a game which puts me on my mettle, which makes me keep my wits about me, which forces me to meet and beat new problems."

In 1924, he brought out his first complete, mahogany-boxed radio sets, the Model 20. That year he spent the extraordinary sum of $500,000 for advertising, $190,000 of it in national magazines. Later Kent's advertising budget would grow to $3 or $4 million a year. The Atwater Kent Radio

Hour on Sunday evening, featuring top singers, cost him $7,000 a week.

In May, 1925, Kent got some valuable publicity when he went up in a dirigible aircraft in New Jersey and broadcast by radio to Mabel, who sat listening on a receiving set he had installed in their car in Lakeside, New Jersey. The U.S. navy pilots of the craft took him over his plant in Philadelphia.

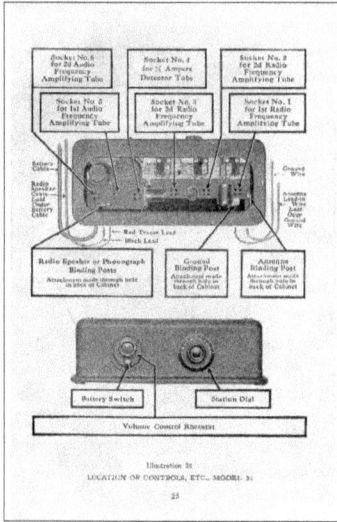

PAGE FROM THE
INSTRUCTION BOOKLET
FOR THE MODEL 35.

He introduced extra power for loudspeakers and amplification for selectivity in urban areas where the airwaves were crowded. In 1926 he introduced Model 20 Compact, which compressed all the various components into a compact space, half the volume of previous models. "Kent's judgment of the public taste was, as usual, accurate," said Alan Douglas, historian of radio manufacturing in the United States. Prior to 1926 it was necessary to adjust three dials to tune in a station. Kent solved this problem on Model 30 by connecting the three tuning condensers with a pulley and drive belt. He received a patent for the invention. Kent's one-millionth set was an even more compact Model 35, boxed in a metal case. Cost-price figures for this model showed the tremendous profit potential in radio manufacture. The Model 35 cost $12 to build and sold for $70.

ATWATER KENT RADIO

Radio needn't disturb any room

Here is a Radio set which simply *melts* into the decorations of any room.

This Atwater Kent Model 20 Compact is as small as a row of a dozen books, as unobtrusive as a well trained servant, as neat and workmanlike as every fine electrical instrument should be.

Yet nothing in effectiveness has been sacrificed in designing this set. The parts in the Model 20 Compact are identical with the parts in the regular Atwater Kent Model 20, rearranged to save space.

Perhaps you still think of Radio as a tangle of wires and untidy parts—to be relegated to the cellar or the attic. But now Radio, thanks to this set, has moved into the rooms where the family lives. It fits naturally into its surroundings. It has actually become decorative as well as entertaining!

Hear the Atwater Kent Radio *Artists* every Thursday evening at 9 o'clock (eastern standard time) through stations:—

WEAF . . . *New York* WEEI . . . *Boston* WCAE . . . *Pittsburgh*
WJAR . . . *Providence* WGR . . . *Buffalo* WOC . . . *Davenport*
WFI . . . *Philadelphia* WWJ . . . *Detroit* WSAI . . . *Cincinnati*
WCCO . . . *Minneapolis-St. Paul*

Write for illustrated booklet telling the story of Atwater Kent Radio.

ATWATER KENT MANUFACTURING COMPANY
A. Atwater Kent, President
4743 Wissahickon Avenue · Philadelphia, Pennsylvania

43

ONE MILLION RADIOS

HE ATWATER KENT MANUFACTURING Co. produced its one millionth radio on Dec. 3, 1926. The two millionth radio was made less than two years later, on Oct. 24, 1928 and was later given to President Herbert Hoover who thanked Kent warmly for it. Kent told "The Talking Machine Journal" of December, 1928 that the rapid production growth "tells the story of radio more graphically than any words could tell it. Nothing has ever so caught the imagination of the American people within such a short space of time and brought to them a utility for practical advancement within social, cultural, business, professional and recreational relationships."

In 1927 when RCA devised the right tubes, it became possible to run radio sets on alternating current, plugged into the wall, getting rid of messy batteries. Just a month after RCA introduced its own Radiola 17 model, the Kent 36 appeared, followed by the 37, "a bombshell in the industry" as it was half the size of the Radiola and cost $88 to the Radiola's $130. The Atwater Kent became the best-selling radio on the market. In 1927 he had 5,000 workers and produced 600,000 sets. In 1929, 8,500 workers produced a million radios.

44

PRODUCING RADIO PARTS, SOME WIRES
SMALLER THAN A HUMAN HAIR

Kent sales that year totaled $60 million. .

In 1928 Kent said that the manufacture of radio sets had matured so that "research and production have supplanted theory and experiment." He said that efficient production had made it possible to sell high quality sets for one-half the price formerly paid. But there was still innovation. Kent introduced one set with a clock device which turned on the radio at the right time to pre-tuned stations.

In May, 1929 he introduced a new Model 55, a screen-grid radio, saying it was "the best that has yet been offered to the public," superior in range, selectivity and tone. He employed skillful publicists, one of whom wrote in a press release that the new product had "new power to reach far away stations, new needlepoint sensitivity to separate the stations and velvety depths of tonal perception."

After buying the Model 55 chassis, the buyer could choose from an array of highboy, lowboy, table and desk-type cabinets of handsome but austere designs reflecting Kent's Vermont background. They could be color coordinated to match the home's décor.

In his first year, Kent had produced 6,000 radios. At the peak of production in 1930 and 1931, Kent produced 6,000 radios a day, an annual rate of two million radios, and his plant employed 12,000 workers. It was the world's largest radio factory and Kent, at 54, was a national figure. A story was told about one namedropper who thought that Atwater Kent was two persons and tried to impress a friend by telling him that he was a close friend of "both Mr. Atwater and Mr. Kent."

BUDDING TYCOON

PATRON OF THE ARTS

S HE BUILT HIS RADIO BUSINESS, Kent emerged as a patron of the arts. As a radio manufacturer and a music lover he saw the huge role music played in early radio programming, perhaps two thirds of the total. He began a tradition of support for the musical arts in 1925 when he financed a series of 30 Sunday night concerts by opera and other musical stars on the radio network of the American Telephone and Telegraph Co. which reached most large cities. Kent hired artists from the Metropolitan Opera company and Victor and Brunswick Talking Machine companies to take part.

ARTICLE IN LITERARY
DIGEST, JANUARY 7, 1928.

The baritone Reinald Werrenrath, star of the first concert, said at the time, "I don't think a more significant thing has happened in the musical world." The New York Times, in an editorial, said that Kent would have to "pay a pretty penny" for the shows even though other radio manufacturers would benefit from them as much as he. The public, said the Times, "would rejoice to get some really first-class singers." The series debuted at 9:15 p.m. on Dec. 4, 1925 and was described in the Times art page as "one of the real treats of the Fall and Winter radio season."

U.S. Secretary of Labor J.J. Davis praised Kent's initiative and said he wondered "if any single force had ever possessed such powers of spreading good." He said most people did not have the opportunity to get to operas or concerts held in the big cities. "But now science has wiped out the distance. It has torn down the walls of the concert hall and opera house. The whole world is one open opera house... and the magic is brought to us as we sit in our homes."

Between Werrenrath's numbers, which included concert pieces, three songs of the sea, and Kipling's "Gunga Din" set to music, Kent went on the air and spoke of his satisfaction to be able to sponsor the series. Later he told a reporter that, as a result of the series, "I have found that the American public likes good music. They will get more of it."

In 1925, Kent started a campaign of support for using radio for educational purposes. "The time will come when every schoolroom – city and country alike – will have a radio receiving set to supplement the work of the teacher in the classroom," he said. In 1928 Kent sent a letter to the Federal Radio Commission asking them to convene a meeting of radio industry and educational leaders to work out a practical program to use radio for educational purposes.

ATWATER KENT
NATIONAL RADIO
AUDITION MEDAL

Kent announced in 1927 that his foundation would conduct annual national radio auditions to identify promising under-25 amateur singers and reward them with $17,500 in cash prizes plus scholarships. Two winners, one male and one female would each receive the Atwater Kent gold medal, $5,000 in cash, and a two-year scholarship at a musical conservatory. Runners-up would receive $2,000 and a one-year scholarship, third places $1,000 and a one-year scholarship, with smaller cash awards for fourth and fifth places.

A writer in Literary Digest commented after the

first contest that "the cause of music might it would seem, be better served by reversing the awards since the third best will naturally need more time and money to bring their efforts to perfection. However to him that hath shall be given."

Some 50,000 entrants from all over the country were winnowed down in state and regional contests to 10 finalists. The first winners, in December 1927, were Agnes Davis, a 24-year-old soprano from Denver and Wilbur W. Evans, a 22-year-old bass-baritone from Philadelphia. The finals were broadcast over a radio network and the finalists feted at banquets in New York. All expenses were picked up by Atwater Kent.

A newspaper in Springfield, Massachusetts, the Republican, commented, "It has been generally accepted that the project, whatever incidental benefits might accrue to the radio concern promoting it, was a sincere effort to discover and help unknown young singers of talent."

The contest continued in future years to much praise. In 1928 winners were Hazel Arth of Washington, D.C., daughter of a member of the U.S. Marine band, and Donald Novis son of a shoestore owner in Pasadena, Calif. Novis went on to a success singing in movies, appearing in such films as "Monte Carlo" starring Jeanette MacDonald in 1930.

TO THE WHITE HOUSE

U. S. PRESIDENTS RECOGNIZED THE PROGRAM. In 1927 Calvin Coolidge called the auditions "a laudable undertaking." And in December of that year he received the 10 finalists and the Kents, including Atwater, Jr. and Elizabeth at the White House. In a diary entry about the visit, Mabel was particularly impressed to be picked up and taken to the White House by Mrs. Edward McLean who was wearing the Hope Diamond, third largest in the world and "the size of a silver dollar," along with a crown of diamonds and "the most gorgeous bracelet I have ever seen." The Coolidges greeted them and "Mrs C. was so gracious and adorable," telling Mabel she had enjoyed meeting 17-year-old Elizabeth, "your cute little red-haired girl." Mabel sat between Andrew Mellon, secretary of the Treasury and Alex Moore, a former ambassador to Spain. Mabel said she watched Mr. Coolidge who, living up to his taciturn reputation, "was very quiet."

In 1929 President Herbert Hoover hosted the 10 finalists, along with Kent and his family, at a White House dinner. Kent, Mabel, Atwater Jr., and Elizabeth also spent the night.

In 1932 the audition had a record number of entries, more than 50,000. The New York Times, in an editorial Aug. 5 of that year said the winners were being rewarded with more than money and scholarships. "The prestige accompanying victory led one baritone to an engagement with the Detroit Civic Opera Company. One of the winners is now leading tenor for a national network studio. Several others, both men and women, are under contract to large radio stations and a number are succeeding in concert work." The Times said that a number of great musical artists of the world have shown their approval by taking part in the judging and in support of winners.

One of the judges in 1932, a foreign opera star, told an interviewer he was surprised that contestants confined themselves to singing opera music. "Why did not one of these young people have the vision to sing "Old Black Joe"? The effect of some simple song would have been electric against such an array of operatic arias."

KENT OUTSIDE THE WHITE HOUSE

Kent himself did not restrict his music appreciation to high-brow singing. He liked and included popular music and hymns in programming he encouraged and controlled. "The good old hymns never die," Kent said in 1930. "We made one hymn part of our first Sunday evening broadcast four years ago and we have closed our Sunday evening concerts with the hymns ever since. The old hymns have a distinct place in American music and will live always."

MANUFACTURING GENIUS

O thers had contributed the basic ideas in the science of radio. Kent, however, contributed efficient mass production and brilliant marketing. He became one of the few American manufacturers to make high-quality products in great quantity. He put engineering brilliance, an unusual energy level and fierce attention to detail to work in creating a plant which was a model of efficiency despite its huge size. Kent was a hands-on captain who ran a tight ship with no bureaucracy. One journalist visitor reported an incident in which Kent was told that a subordinate was preparing a long report and would soon have it ready. "What's the matter with him," Kent was quoted as saying. "Has he suddenly become speechless? Why can't he come in here and tell me what he has found out. I don't want to read over a long report."

KENT IN THE TOOL ROOM
OF HIS FACTORY

The sales force was educated and motivated by an in-house manual "Making Sales" which told salesmen that they were "perhaps the strongest and most important link in the whole chain of manufacturing and distribution." Franklin Atlee, who worked in the Atwater Kent Mfg. Co. sales department for ten years, 1923-33, said that Kent's promotional efforts were a key to the success

The Factory Behind the Product

The building shown on the left was the largest Radio Factory in the world. Now, with the addition of the building on the right, it is doubly the largest—its total floor space covering 32 acres. This is a greater area than would be covered by 28 football fields.

ATWATER KENT MFG COMPANY
4700 Wissahickon Avenue
Philadelphia

of the radios. Retired in Florida, he told the St. Petersburg Times that Kent "worked very closely with his engineers, designers and draftsmen from beginning to end, and he was very insistent that the final product be exactly to his liking." Atlee described Kent as possessed of unusual health and vigor, with sparkling eyes and a springy step and said he exhibited "friendly recognition of his workers."

Kent was ahead of his time in trying to get the most out of his workers. The Talking Machine Journal of January, 1925 said Kent encouraged employees to think while working and make suggestions for improvements, many of which were valuable. He was known for treating his employees well by all contemporary standards. In 1925 he personally financed a Welfare Fund to tide over workers who were temporarily laid off because of demand fluctuation. In the depression years following the 1929 Crash, Kent had to let workers go. But in 1931 he started a program to help workers laid off after the crash who had worked for him at least one year. According to the Philadelphia Bulletin, he was supporting 3,500 laid off workers with fuel and food. "This work has given me more genuine satisfaction than anything I have done for a long time," Kent told the paper.

The Talking Machine Journal said that branches of his organization functioned without his supervision but, if in doubt, could get an instant, definite decision from Kent. "He believes in doing something, right or wrong, abhorring the thought of anyone doing nothing, in preference to activity, for fear of being in error," the magazine said. Kent's management approach followed the later advice of Yogi Berra: "If you come to a fork in the road, take it."

Factory and office lighting was excellent and offices were placed so supervisors could keep an eye on the manufacturing floor. Kent had his own office suite in the plant including dressing room, kitchen and dining room. A reporter from the New York Times in 1927 wrote, "everything keeps moving ahead on conveyor belts. Production is speeded up in every way. If two holes are to be bored, one man bores one while another man is boring the other. You see girls winding wire that can scarcely be seen with the naked eye since it is thinner than a human hair... Practically everything that goes into the sets is made before your eyes."... Tremendously big machines are used "with hardly an operator in sight." One out of every ten employees is an inspector, testing the work of others. "Each set receives 150 tests." "Flooded with daylight, the establishment is kept so clean that practically everybody can wear good clothes...the executives appear unusually youthful." An unusual aspect of the enterprise was that all Kent employees, workers and executives, except for a skeleton staff, took vacation at the same time.

A costly frill was the 14-carat gold plating on each Atwater Kent nameplate attached to the radio sets. At the plant, visitors could watch through a special window to see gold bars dissolving to make the plating. One visitor asked why. "Mr. Kent ordered it," was the reply.

Kent became the leader in the radio manufacturing industry despite intense competition from some 200 other manufacturers including great firms such as RCA, Westinghouse and Zenith. Patent lawsuits were frequent. In 1927, Kent settled a suit brought by RCA under which Kent would pay RCA royalties amounting to 7.5% of the value of all sets sold since 1923 and in the future, ending several years of litigation over patents on radio tubes. David Sarnoff, general manager of RCA, said the settlement would allow both firms "to spend more time selling receiving sets and less time in the courts."

Historian Douglas said that Kent, had he pressed the case, might have beaten RCA in which case RCA's licensing structure would have disintegrated. RCA made a deal with Kent on the above terms but Douglas says, "it is unlikely that the Atwater Kent Co. ever paid any back royalties and quite possible that it paid less than 7.5% later." The exact license terms will probably never be known since Kent destroyed his company records when he closed his plant and retired in 1936, Douglas said.

THE CRASH

ORMALLY INAUGURATING HIS EXPANDED PLANT IN MAY 1929, Kent said the factory was concrete evidence of his confidence in the future of radio. "Great as the success of radio has been in the past, I feel more confident than ever that its greatest development lies in the future," Kent told an audience of Philadelphia leaders. Like most Americans he did not see the ugly storm clouds on the horizon. Five months later, in "Black October," the U.S. stock market crashed and started the longest and most severe depression in the history of the Western democracies. In one month, stocks fell 40%. By 1932, the value of all stock was one-fifth its 1929 level. In the same period 11,000 of the 25,000 banks in the country closed, farm income dropped two-thirds and manufacturing output was cut in half. About 15 million were unemployed, 25% of the work force.

The depression did not spare the market for high-quality radio sets. Kent's factory was down to 1,500 workers by 1933 despite a switch to moderately priced models. Atwater, Jr., on a business trip to Texas, wrote his father in 1931 that dealers were clamoring for a "midget" set. But Kent refused to enter the growing market for cheap sets eventually dominated by Philco. To make use of spare factory capacity Kent began manufacturing refrigerators in 1934.

A paternalistic owner, Kent also resisted the unionization trend. Kent had built his business virtually by himself and he refused to relax his one-man control. But in the Depression the unions were gaining strength. In

1933 the American Federation of Radio Workers tried to organize his plant and several hundred workers walked out. The dispute was settled with a 10 percent pay raise and Kent told the unions not to come back. They did, in 1936, making new demands which, to say the least, turned out to be counterproductive.

That month, news appeared which Radio Weekly declared was "the most sensational news, in all likelihood, that has ever broken in the macabre radio industry." Atwater Kent was getting out of radio.

KENT IN KENNEBUNKPORT

WHY KENT QUIT RADIO

*H*IS COMPANY ANNOUNCED JUNE 3, "Atwater Kent Manufacturing Co. has decided to be less active in radio lines." In fact, all production had ceased and sales were from sets on hand. Kent refused an offer from 20 managers to buy him out, destroyed his company records, let the last 800 workers go, and walked away.

Radio Weekly reported that "Mr. Kent is known to view the possibility of profitable operation in radio very dubiously and, as the possessor of a large personal fortune, he is believed to be preparing for a period of rest and recreation."

That was only one reason. Kent was known to dislike intensely the policies of Franklin Roosevelt's New Deal and some family members speculated that this was an important reason for his abandonment of the radio business.

Kent's orderly, forward-looking mind would also have foreseen that even when the economic depression ended, radio would be overwhelmed by television. By the early 1930's television existed in research laboratories. David Sarnoff of RCA predicted in 1931 that it would be commercialized by 1933. He said RCA already had transmitting stations in New York City and a subsidiary, the National Broadcasting Corp., was preparing to broadcast. He was too optimistic. The depression and World War Two delayed the development of television. But radio was on the eve of taking a back seat when Kent quit.

At 63 he had amassed, in cash and investments alone, a fortune he estimated at more than $42 million. Millions more were in the value of his plants, residential real estate and personal property. His fortune, adjusted for inflation, would be the equivalent in today's dollars of more than $500 million.

In the 1938 memo to his son, Kent said he was satisfied with the money he had made. He had resisted pressure "from hundreds of brokers and promoters" to cash in further by selling stock to the public during the 1920's stock trading frenzy. He could have doubled his fortune at least by selling stock. But he told his son, "I did not care to have the brokers sell at high prices, stock bearing the 'Atwater Kent' name, which probably later would not pay the stockholder the dividends they were looking for and the purchasers would, naturally, have blamed me for not giving them a 'square deal.' I have never regretted not having the Atwater Kent stock sold to the public." His refusal to sell stock to the public also gave Kent absolute freedom to dispose of his company as he saw fit.

Kent never gambled on the stock market during the 1920's. He kept his millions mostly in cash in banks in Philadelphia. He told his son that at the time of the crash his financial position was the strongest "of any individual in the city."

It is likely that all these factors played a role in Kent's decamping: union pressure, falling demand for radios, resentment at the New Deal, the future of television, unwillingness to start over in a new field, great wealth and the temptation of a comfortable retirement. He had the satisfaction of knowing that he was leaving behind a reputation for quality products still reflected in the enthusiasm of collectors. John P. Wolkonowitz wrote in the Worcester Polytechnic Institute alumni magazine in 1976, "More often than not, even after 40 years of storage, an Atwater Kent will operate perfectly at the first click of the switch."

Characteristically, Kent never wavered in his decision to quit business. He sold one of his two plants to the General Motors affiliate, Bendix Aviation Corp. in 1940 for $1 million. The other plant, a building with 24 acres of floor space, and 20 adjacent acres of land, was first leased to

Sears, Roebuck and Co. for mail order operations and, in 1941, sold to the U.S. Signal Corps for $2 million. After the war it was taken over by the Veterans Administration. In 1977, as part of an inner-city revitalization project, the plant was refurbished with $6 million in state and federal grants into the Wissahickon Industrial Center to house small businesses.

PRIVATE LIFE

*T*t had not been all work and no play for Kent during the great radio manufacturing years. One Kent pastime was buying real estate, for his own estates and as an investment. During the 1920's, in addition to his own $4 million suburban Philadelphia estate, "West Hills," near the Merion Golf Club, he assembled "Foxcroft" a 750-acre property near Bryn Mawr, much of it used for foxhunting by the Radnor Hunt Club. He announced plans to subdivide and develop the property in 1937 to provide for as many as 400 residences.

In 1927, Kent bought "Sonogee" an estate on Frenchmans Bay in Bar Harbor, Maine from Frederick Vanderbilt. A year later he bought the

"SONOGEE," BAR HARBOR, MAINE

"The Towers," Palm Beach, Florida

The Kents in Kennebunkport

KENT AND A DAUGHTER, BOATING IN MAINE

KENT'S CARS AT "WEST HILLS"

THE KENTS WITH THEIR ROLLS ROYCE

neighboring estate "Brookend", from Dr. Robert Abbe, a New York surgeon. In the same period he bought an Addison Mizner-designed mansion in Palm Beach, Florida. In April, 1929 he bought Brookthorpe Farms, an 800-acre property in Delaware County in the Philadelphia suburbs for $2.5 million. A Delaware County estate of more than 100 acres, with a mansion and farm buildings, was given as a wedding present to his daughter Elizabeth and her husband, William Van Alen.

In an article on his retirement, Time described Kent's social life: "For years the Kents have gone to Bar Harbor every summer, to Palm Beach every winter. Kent yachts ply all the waters from Maine to Florida. The Kent garages must be big enough to hold a score of cars for Mr. Kent dislikes driving the same car two days in succession."

In fact, at their peak, the garages sheltered 32 cars. Atwater Kent, Jr., an avid sailor, kept a list of Kent-owned yachts which included the motor boats "Mabeth" at 40 feet, "Virbet" at 80 feet, "Alondra" at 162 feet, "Whileaway" at 177 feet and two dozen smaller craft. The 800-ton Whileaway, bought in 1931 from Harry Payne Whitney, had cabin space for 50 guests. Kent sold Whileaway to a South American buyer before WW II and sadly the yacht ended up as a sub tender for German submarines in the Caribbean.

PRIVATE LIFE

THE NOVELIST KENNETH ROBERTS, a family friend, wrote a friendly spoof of Kent's lifestyle in the form of a playlet which he sent to Mabel in 1935. After a hilarious exchange between Mabel and Atwater about how many spare butlers are needed (120), Atwater Jr. appears and asks if he can take the yacht "Majestic" for a trip to Newfoundland with friends. The play continues:

Mr. Kent (thoughtfully) – I am sorry Atwater but I decided this morning to have the turbines of the Majestic overhauled. I am using the Calisthenic myself for a trip to Bermuda; and your mother is going to take the Rheumatic for a cruise to Kennebunkport, because the Myers are having a picnic on the rocks.

Atwater – How about the Neurotic, father?

KENT'S 177-FOOT YACHT, "WHILEAWAY"

Mr. Kent – *The gyroscopic stabilizer of the Neurotic is out of order, Atwater. Let me see. There is the Plethoric and the Caloric and the Harmonic and the Cathartic, there you are, Atwater, the Cathartic! The captain has just had a two-month's vacation and the twelve B-Deck staterooms have been redecorated by Charles of London. How large a party did you wish to take?*

Atwater – *I thought I'd take about forty, father.*

Mr. Kent (indulgently) – *Forty would make a nice little party, Atwater. All of you could get on B and C decks and you would only need to use outside staterooms with bath.*

Atwater – *Very well, father.*

Mr. Kent – *I will speak to the steward and see that he takes plenty of fresh caviar and a lot of can openers.*

(Later...)

Mr. Kent (as savagely as is possible for him) – *And Atwater, I wish you to see Prentiss at once and tell him he is not to use the Pthisic any more. A two hundred and fifty foot yacht is altogether too large for that boy to handle; and if he keeps on doing it, we will wake up one morning and find that he has run it up on land and into our living room, and then your mother would probably want to leave it there so we could have picnics on it.*

LAUNCHING THE DAUGHTERS

ENT WAS DESCRIBED BY TIME MAGAZINE IN 1936 as "suave, affable, approachable but highly individualistic." He maintained his rural Vermont manners as he grew in wealth and sophistication. During a 1937 visit by Atwater Kent to Calais, Louise Andrews Kent, journalist wife of Kent's second cousin Ira Rich Kent, noted this. She wrote her husband, "I enjoyed At's visit very much. He certainly has a lot of charm. I think you missed the spot when Hector (apparently a rustic neighbor) came up on the porch and At offered him his chair. Hector took it leaving At roosting on the rail."

While indulging in yachts, estates and servants, and giving generously to charity, Kent also pinched pennies. Ira Rich Kent, an executive with the publishing firm of Houghton Miflin in Boston, wrote to his mother in 1929 when Kent was selling 6,000 radios a day, that he was having trouble collecting $2,500 he had lent Atwater. "At, like many people of wealth, is not always easy to collect from, although I am sure he is certain." Another Kent cousin Dorman, grandson of Abdiel Kent, wrote in his May 10, 1919 dairy entry that Atwater had sent him $100 for his help in making funeral arrangements for Atwater's father, Dr. Prentiss Kent. "I nearly fell dead," Dorman wrote.

By the middle of the 1930's the three older children were grown. Atwater, Jr. was prominent in sailing circles with his sleek 12-meter sloop "Arundel." The two girls were married after what Time magazine described as a friendly competition among Philadelphia tycoons to present their

THE KENT FAMILY:
VIRGINIA, ATWATER JR., PRENTISS,
MABEL, ATWATER, & ELIZABETH

daughters to eligible young men: "Philadelphia is still chuckling over the days when Mr. Kent, Clarence Henry Geist (United Gas Improvement) and the late John T. Dorrance (Campbell Soup) had a baseball team of marriageable daughters between them,' Time wrote in 1936. "In the competitive spending which the launching of these nine young women entailed, the Dorrance triumph was a "Jungle Ball" in Philadelphia's Bellevue Stratford Hotel where the ballroom was realistically decorated with coconut palms, tanks of tropical fish, a menagerie of monkeys, apes, bears, snakes and hundreds of birds singing in cages hung from the ceiling. Geist's big play was a party on his suburban estate, where 20 acres were converted into a "Versailles Garden" with electric stars in the shrubs. Mr. Kent waited until summer, then gave not one, but two balls simultaneously at his Bar Harbor estate. One was on a yacht, the other on shore. Flower-bedecked launches carried guests back and forth."

In 1931, Kent's oldest daughter, Elizabeth, married William Van Alen, an architect from an old New York family connected to the Astors and Vanderbilts and they settled, with three children, in "Rushton" the estate they acquired from Kent. The younger daughter, Virginia, married Cummins Catherwood, a wealthy Philadelphia businessman.

DIVORCE

*A*t the time Kent made his break with the business his marriage was also breaking up. When Mabel sued for divorce in 1940, she cited "indignities" beginning in 1928. But even after the alleged indignities began (presumably adultery on Kent's part) she had worked hard to keep the marriage together. Her letters in the early 1930's, when he had become a major tycoon and was often away, were affectionate. In one 1931 letter she started "Dearest" and said "after hearing your sweet voice, I felt like a new human being."

Kent was never a Jazz Age playboy. But with great wealth pouring in, he did not remain faithful. Family members were told later that Kent had secretly installed a mistress in a house near his Bar Harbor mansion. In 1923, Atwater and Mabel adopted a newborn baby boy and named him after Kent's father, Prentiss. His origin was a family mystery. Kent's name was linked in tabloids with that of a noted society beauty, a Mrs. Thompson. Some papers left to his son, Atwater, included a few love letters written to Kent in the late 1930's addressed to "Dear Nunkey" from a woman in England who signed herself "Vivi." In what was apparently an early "palimony" case, he was sued in the early 1940's by a woman identified only as "Vivian." "My lawyers say she will receive practically nothing," Kent wrote Atwater, Jr. in 1943, but he apologized for the unwelcome publicity.

In 1938 the Kents took separate vacations, Atwater to Bar Harbor and Mabel to Kennebunkport, Maine. The Philadelphia Bulletin quoted

Mabel as saying the separation would be "an opportunity to rest." The rest was permanent; Kent moved out in 1939. In September 1940, Mabel sued for divorce. After legal diplomacy they were granted a divorce "a mensa et thoro", meaning a formal separation, in Delaware County, Pa.

She spent the rest of her life supported in comfort in her homes in Philadelphia, Florida and Maine, a beloved matriarch known to her children and ten grandchildren as "Gan."

Louise Kent, writer wife of Atwater's cousin Ira Rich Kent, caught the essence of Mabel's warmth in a letter to her husband after a 1936 visit to Philadelphia. "Mabel is a darling," she wrote, describing how Mrs. Kent had come in to her guest room after dinner "lay down beside me on top of the satin blanket cover in the clubbiest way and we talked for

MABEL AND ATWATER AT "SONOGEE," BAR HARBOR, 1936

a long time." Mabel told Louise that if she was a good person it was no credit to her, that people always did after all what they liked best to do. "What Mabel likes best to do is to be kind to people," Louise said.

Mabel was an exception in an age when people did not express their deep personal feelings easily. But she did not confide in her children about what caused the break. Kent was for many years a generous, thoughtful husband. He was always described as considerate to others. An interviewer from the Shrine Magazine wrote in 1927 that Kent was "painstakingly neat in personal appearance and polite as an ambassador." His children loved him. Elizabeth, visiting Paris at 18, called him "the dearest of dear

Daddys" in a 1928 letter.

But he was also self-contained, unemotional and highly independent. Perhaps the momentous decision to take his chips off the table in business brought an urge for a wider break including his marital ties. There is also the possibility that, in an age of untamed male chauvinism, he wanted to have his cake and eat it too, maintaining his marriage and his mistresses. And Mabel put her foot down.

Mabel did not forget her husband. She told family members that not long after World War Two she sat next to a businessman at dinner in Palm Beach. The man "had eyes like At's," she said. Impressed, she phoned the office which handled family investments and instructed them to buy shares in the man's fledgling business machine company. They followed her wishes but weeks later, unwilling to stick with Mabel's hunch, the investment managers sold the shares. Too bad for Mabel. Her dinner partner had been Thomas Watson, founder of IBM.

CALIFORNIA'S
"MR. HOST"

*I*N 1939, KENT BOUGHT A 14-ACRE ESTATE, "Villa Maria" in Southampton, Long Island with an 18-room mansion including a frieze from the Toronia Palace in Rome. But by 1942 he had settled in California in a 32-room Italian villa, Capo di Monte, on 12 acres at Los Angeles' highest point, a hilltop in the posh suburb of Bel Air. In 1943 he left Philadelphia and Maine mansions to his wife, sold "Sonogee" and the Southampton and Florida mansions and became a California resident.

CAPO DI MONTE

Capo di Monte was surrounded with gardens, fish ponds, sculpture and a swimming pool. It had a breathtaking view over the city and the blue Pacific. When it was sold after his death, the ad described it: "Magnificent 12-acres fully landscaped with commanding view, 7 master bed rooms, 5 baths, 2 sitting rooms, 2 dressing rooms, sun porch, large living room, music room, game room,, powder and men's room, pantry, kitchen, servants' dining room, store room, 6 servants' rooms, 3 baths, salon. Two guest apartments, 3 rooms and bath each. 5-car garage. Large tile swimming pool, heated. Tennis court."

Kent loved the house and California. He wrote his son in 1943 that he was sold on California and its climate, unlike Philadelphia where people are chased out by the heat in the summer and the cold in the winter. "Here at Capo di Monte I can stay the entire 12 months and not be uncomfortable enough to want to go anywhere else ... out here one can stay just where one lives and find tremendously interesting things to do."

ATWATER KENT (CENTER) WITH STAFF AND ENTERTAINERS AT HIS "CIRCUS" PARTY, CAPO DI MONTE, C. 1945

What he found to do was to become what Life magazine called "Hollywood's most fabulous host." Helped by a domestic staff of 17, including a full-time flower arranger, he began giving non-stop lunches, dinners and dances for groups from a guest list of the movie colony's top stars and socialites.

LARAINE DAY AND ELIZABETH TAYLOR AT KENT'S "CIRCUS" PARTY, C. 1945

"Often he does not remember all his guests names, but they have no trouble recognizing the genial little millionaire who likes to dress up very much like the Mad Hatter and see that everyone has a lovely time," wrote Life which several times took its readers via the photo lens to visit Kent's parties. Life's 1946 visit pictured a lunch attended by Viscount Lascelles, Princess Pigniatelli and Baron Maurice de Rothschild among others. A buffet dinner included Van Johnson, Robert Stack, June Haver, John Payne and Gloria DeHaven. The Cholly Knickerbocker gossip column reported that at one Hollywood party, Paramount public relations man Bob Taplinger announced he was the only man in Hollywood who had never been invited to an Atwater Kent party. Another guest suggested that Taplinger should be exhibited at the Los Angeles museum as "one of Hollywood's greatest rarities."

The actor David Niven gave a melancholy picture of Kent as party giver in his memoir, "Bring On the Empty Horses." Niven said guests were treated to beluga caviar, French champagne and the best of everything. But many of them never saw their host, "an eccentric and lonely little old millionaire," because "he usually took refuge in a huge leather wing chair in a remote library and stayed there all night."

"If occasionally the better-mannered would go to the remote library to seek out Atwater Kent and thank him, he was almost pathetically touched, smiled a wispy little smile, and marked them down in his heart as 'friends.' When he departed this earth, he left bequests to 73 'friends' and enjoined them to use the money 'for happiness,' something, perhaps, he had always been short of," Niven said.

The New York Daily Mirror, in a portrait of Kent written after his death in 1949, wrote: "Downstairs in his mansion the Hollywood stars, whose friendship he'd coveted, frolicked by the hundreds even as Mr. Host of Hollywood was dying. They gorged themselves on his imported foods. They lapped up his champagne. They fell into his turquoise-tiled swimming pool. Few bothered to inquire into Atty's absence from the gay scene."

James Carter the writer of the Daily mirror portrait quoted a prominent New York psychiatrist, Jacob L. Moreno as saying Kent in Hollywood may have been simply seeking a pat on the back. "When he first went to Hollywood he thought he had realized his adolescent dream, to be a god among gods. But as in all cases of single-minded, isolated geniuses, he found he couldn't buy his made-to-order dreams," Moreno said.

ATWATER KENT AND
HEDDA HOPPER

In contrast to what Niven and Moreno said, Kent seemed to enjoy the new role as Hollywood's "Mr. Host." He spoke freely to gossip columnists, particularly Hedda Hopper and Cobina Wright who were close friends. The parties were recorded by a professional photographer who then prepared albums. One of these, still in the family, was titled "Atwater Kent's Ideal Party" and had pictures of Kent and guests Alan Ladd, Dorothy Lamour, Cornell Wilde, Van Johnson, Kirk Douglas, Loretta Young, Joan Fontaine and other stars. Another album had Kent, in jest, being served a drink by the "butler," British actor Arthur Treacher and sitting on a couch surrounded by four glamorous starlets. A Kent specialty was "circus" parties at which hundreds of guests mingled with elephants, monkeys, clowns and trained dogs. During World War II Kent entertained officers and soldiers, including one party for 10 officers of the French underground. A newspaper reported a head count of 1738 guests at one Kent party.

ATWATER KENT AND
LORETTA YOUNG

Cobina Wright, a New York socialite, opera singer and actress, who was a prominent figure on the Hollywood scene with her own gossip column, was a close friend of Kent's. In her autobiography, "I Never Grew Up," she described Kent as "a very shy, gray little man, always a kind of shadowy figure at his own feasts." She said the 5'5" host was often distracted and described how she went to a cocktail party at his house to cheer herself up after her mother's funeral. Kent greeted her warmly and she told him her mother had just died. "How charming," he replied. But she said that, along with William Randolph Hearst's mistress Marian Davies, Kent was one of Hollywood's two outstanding hosts who genuinely enjoyed giving pleasure to others. "Only at his parties could he stand by and observe any happiness that his money brought, and for that reason they were personal to him, and he enjoyed them more than any single person I have ever known," Wright wrote.

On the question of whether he was happy or lonely in California, maybe the answer is both. It cannot have been particularly stimulating to him to have as his primary concern which movie star to sit next to which socialite. But Kent had the sense to realize that this is a retirement dilemma most would envy. He chose it and with his habit of not questioning his own decisions, he felt content. David Niven's conclusion that Kent was lonely depends on one's definition of the word. Kent was not lonely in the sense that he was alone. He was surrounded by beautiful people. But there is no evidence that he had any close friends. He had only acquaintances, many who genuinely liked him, some who adored him, but no one he needed to be around. He seemed content with his own company, visits from his children, and the glamorous backdrop.

The September, 1946 issue of "Screen Guide" wrote that Kent's parties provided a useful service in bringing together all social groups. "All Hollywood goes to Mr. Kent's parties," the magazine wrote. ""His enthusiasm to surround himself with bright young people, regardless of their social standing, has helped break down some of Hollywood's phoney social barriers. Sometimes Mr. Kent gives the parties himself; sometimes he lends his home to friends who lack the space to entertain." His lunch and parties were carefully organized, guests always seated at tables of six which Kent believed ideal for conversation and to avoid risking that Hollywood egos might be ignored at larger tables.

His hospitality extended beyond parties. Kent's son-in-law William Van Alen, an avid tennis player, said that before one visit to Capo di Monte he expressed an interest in getting in some tennis. He arrived to find that Kent had arranged for a match with seven-time Wimbledon champion Helen Wills.

Kent was no wild playboy. Any affairs were discreet. In a town of heavy drinking and drug-use, he was a sober citizen who took an occasional glass of sherry. His pastimes were card-playing and music. Kent was fastidious about his health and diet, avoiding milk, coffee and chocolate, and taking daily vitamins, a monthly "colonic," sun baths or untraviolet ray treatments several times a week and regularly rubbing himself with olive oil to avoid dry skin. He took weekly singing lessons from Mrs. Yeatman Griffth and was described as having "a pleasant baritone." In one photo album he is shown, with a piano accompanist, giving a solo recital for a group of guests. Kent wrote his son in 1944 that he thought the singing "makes me appear and feel younger as it makes me more active."

ATWATER KENT SINGS FOR GUESTS AT CAPO DI MONTE,
FEBRUARY 23, 1945

Kent also took enjoyment in redecorating inside and outside at Capo de Monte. "I find that small, simple and inexpensive changes about a house or grounds keeps one young and alive and gives one great happiness," he wrote to his son. He built a small pool house, glassed in on three sides, "a place I love to go and sit alone, as the scenery is beautiful with the mountains, the canyons, the pool and grounds. When I have been up there and come back to the house I feel I have been off to some distant resort."

CHARITY

$\mathscr{H}$E CONTINUED GIVING AWAY MONEY GENEROUSLY. His first
recorded gift had been in 1927 when he donated $5,000
to the University of Vermont to help students who showed
promise in electrical engineering.

In 1929, at Helen Keller's request, he began giving radio sets to the
American Foundation for the Blind. In 1930 he gave the then-huge sum
of $220,000 to help build what became the Franklin Institute, a first-
class science and technology museum in Philadelphia. Four years later
he discovered and presented the Institute with a valuable 18th century
statue of Franklin by the French sculptress Marie Suzanne.

In 1936, the year he gave up his radio business, he undertook to
restore the Betsy Ross House in Philadelphia, generally believed to be
the house where George Washington commissioned the widow, Betsy
Griscom Ross, to make the first American flag. Kent provided $25,000 to
rebuild the dilapidated dwelling.

In 1937 he provided $80,000 to modernize the original Franklin
Institute building (the Institute had moved uptown to larger quarters)
and remake it as the Atwater Kent Museum devoted to the history of
Philadelphia. During his life he gave away millions through his Atwater
Kent Foundation.

On his death, Kent left another $1.335 million to charity, divided
between the Atwater Kent Museum, University of Pennsylvania medical
school, Jefferson Medical College, Worcester Polytechnic Institute, Tufts

College, the University of Vermont and Vermont Historical Society, UCLA, and the Southern California symphony orchestra.

He also, as mentioned by David Niven, left $442,000 divided among the 73 Hollywood friends including Greer Garson, Hedda Hopper, Edgar Bergen and Cornell Wilde. Employees also benefited. Kent left $351,000 divided among 11 household servants.

FINALE

KENT DIED ON MARCH 4, 1949 of complications connected with prostate cancer. In the final years before his death, though winding down, he kept up his party giving. In 1947 he attended the Oscar Awards party and wrote to his son, "I had six parties in December, more than I will have again if I can help it. At the time they all seemed to be necessary." In May 1948 he hosted a "Fiesta" bash for 2,000 guests from the National Association of Broadcasters. That fall the parties stopped after Kent fell ill with a virus infection.

In the final weeks before he died, when he was gravely ill, Kent reverted to what some believe was an essentially lonely nature. He received no one except nurses, doctors, a close aide and a secretary.

Nine days before he died he dictated his last letter, to his son Atwater, Jr. It said: "I am sorry that I am lying here in bed and sorry that I cannot see you all, but this makes it impossible. With much love, I am". Kent was too ill even to sign the letter or to read letters sent to him. Six letters written to Kent in his last days by Atwater Jr. were returned unopened.

Kent had never been a regular churchgoer and family members do not remember him discussing religion. But 17 days before he died he dictated a memo for his family and friends indicating that he was thinking about God. "These views you may not agree with at all but I have had them in mind for many years, " he said.

He said he was brought up in the Congregational Church, believed in God and worshipped according to Congregational beliefs. But he said he had changed and described a simple non-theological belief. "Lately, I have come to worship Nature as a symbol of the greatest God that I know. This is caused by realizing the tremendous works that have been done by God in the universe in the last 350,000,000 years. I also recognize by comparison (presumably to the works of man) the power of God and I want to believe that God is the greatest power in the world visible to the eye."

Despite his lifestyle and the millions given away to charities and already settled on his family, he left fortunes to his wife Mabel, from whom he was legally separated but not divorced, and to his three children, A. Atwater Kent, Jr., Elizabeth Kent Van Alen and Virginia Kent Catherwood.

Kent's Vermont frugality would have been shocked at the haste his executors exhibited selling some of his property after his death. Six months after Kent died, executors hired auctioneer Samuel Freeman to sell 1,200 acres of his suburban Philadelphia property in a three-day auction. A glossy brochure picturing the beautiful properties gushed that "never before has such an acreage been offered at unrestricted public auction and it is to be sold, no matter how low the bids may be." The auction flopped. Total receipts were $900,000, a loss from purchase prices paid in the overheated days of the 1920's and an eventual bonanza for clever buyers. A generation later the land would be worth $10 million or more and today more than $100 million.

His 370-picture art collection, which reportedly cost more than $1 million, also was sold for bargain-basement prices. A Gainsborough portrait of English poet Thomas Chatterton sold for $1,000, a Rubens self-portrait for $950 and a portrait of Lady Cockburn by Sir Joshua Reynolds for $750. The New York Times reporter wrote that "auctioneers groaned as buyers refused to extend themselves" in 90-degree heat of the courtyard at Kent's Bel Air mansion.

Kent did not make the return trip to the hills of his native Vermont for burial. He was interred at Los Angeles' famous Forest Lawn Memorial Park with 200 family and friends in attendance. The style was California, not Vermont. The Florists Review of May1949 reported that a blanket of 1,800 camellias covered the casket, which rested on a catafalque decorated with 600 roses.

ATWATER KENT (1873-1949)
M. (1905) MABEL LUCAS, (1883-1971)

Atwater Kent, Jr. (1908-1988) m. (1941) Denyse Binon (1916-1957), 4 children; m. (1960) Hope Parkhurst (1932-), 2 children	Virginia Kent (1915-1966) m. (1935) Cummins Catherwood (1910-1990)

Virginia Catherwood (1938-)

Suzanne Kent (1942-2013)

Atwater Kent III (1944-)

Christopher Kent (1949-)

Peter Kent (1952-)

Hewlett Kent (1962-)

Allison Kent (1965-)

Elizabeth Kent (1911-2015) m. (1931) William L. Van Alen (1907-2003)

William L. Van Alen, Jr. (1933-2010)

James L. Van Alen II (1935-)

Cassandra Van Alen (1937-)

ATWATER KENT, JR. (1908-1988)
M. (1941) DENYSE BINON (1916-1957)

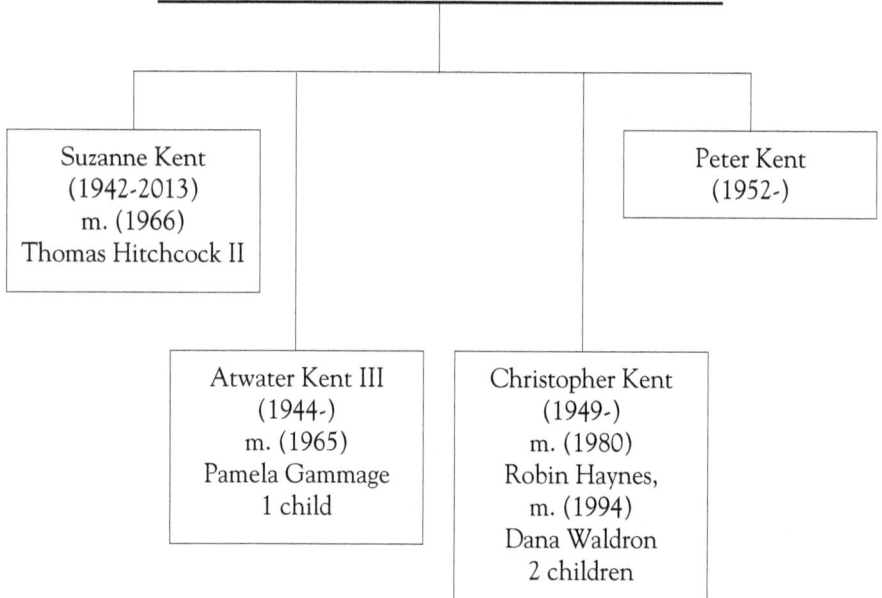

Suzanne Kent
(1942-2013)
m. (1966)
Thomas Hitchcock II

Peter Kent
(1952-)

Atwater Kent III
(1944-)
m. (1965)
Pamela Gammage
1 child

Christopher Kent
(1949-)
m. (1980)
Robin Haynes,
m. (1994)
Dana Waldron
2 children

ATWATER KENT, JR. (1908-1988)
M. (1960) HOPE PARKHURST (1932-)

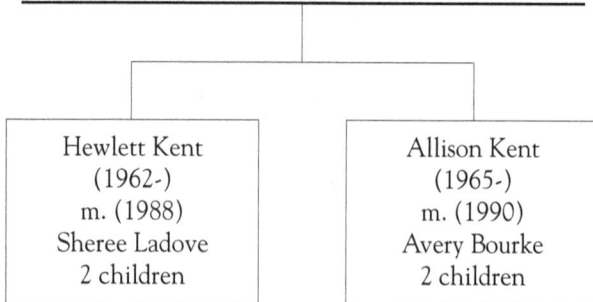

Hewlett Kent
(1962-)
m. (1988)
Sheree Ladove
2 children

Allison Kent
(1965-)
m. (1990)
Avery Bourke
2 children

ELIZABETH KENT (1911-2015)
M. (1931) WILLIAM VAN ALEN, (1907-2003)

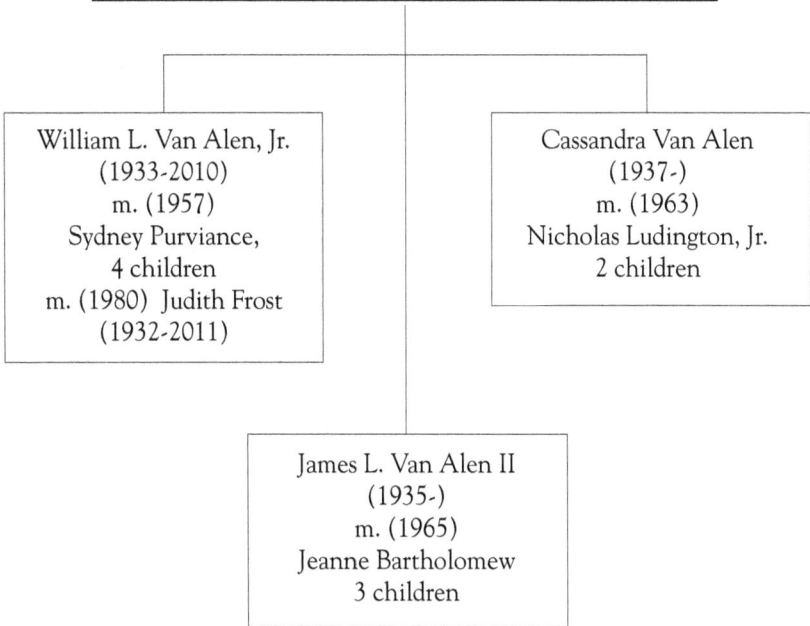

William L. Van Alen, Jr.
(1933-2010)
m. (1957)
Sydney Purviance,
4 children
m. (1980) Judith Frost
(1932-2011)

Cassandra Van Alen
(1937-)
m. (1963)
Nicholas Ludington, Jr.
2 children

James L. Van Alen II
(1935-)
m. (1965)
Jeanne Bartholomew
3 children

VIRGINIA KENT (1915-1966)
M. (1961) CUMMINS CATHERWOOD, (1910-1990)

Virginia Catherwood
(1938-)
m. (1961)
Perry Gresh
(1933-2004)
2 children

Sources

Cate, Weston A., *Forever Calais*, 1999, Barre Vt. (A history of Calais Township)

Douglas, Alan, *Radio Manufacturers of the 1920's*, 1988, Chandler, AZ. (Includes a chapter on Atwater Kent radios.)

Kent, A. Atwater, *Electrical Units for Boys*, 1900, Kendrick and Davis, Lebanon NH.

Kent, A. Atwater, Undated (1938?) Memo to A. Atwater Kent, Jr. on his business career. (In Kent Co. files.)

Kent, Dorman, *Diaries*. Stored at Vermont Historical Society, Montpelier, VT. (Unedited and voluminous daily records.)

Kent, Dorman, Unpublished, undated memo to A. Atwater Kent on Kent ancestors. (In Kent Co. Files.)

Kent, Ira Rich, Letters stored at Vermont Historical Society, Montpelier, VT.

Kent, Mabel Lucas, Prentiss J., A. Atwater, A. Atwater, Jr., Letters stored at Kent Co., Wilmington, Del.

New York Times collection, New York Public Library.

Niven, David, *Bring On the Empty Horses*, New York, 1975.

Periodicals collection, New York Public Library.

Philadelphia Evening Bulletin collection, Urban Archives Center, Paley Library, Temple University.

Van Alen, Elizabeth Kent and William, Interviews 2001.

Williams, Ralph, "Atwater Kent, Master of Marketing," in AWA Review, Volume X, 1996.

Wolkonowicz, John P., "Atwater Kent, The Forgotten Millionaire," WPI Journal, August 1976, Worcester, MA.

Wright, Cobina, *I Never Grew Up*, New York, 1952.

Image Credits

All images in this book are courtesy of the family of Atwater Kent with the exception of the following pages that are courtesy of the Library of Congress: pages 41, 45, 48, 51, 52, 57, 62 (bottom), 63 (top), and 64.

Front cover image courtesy of the Library of Congress.